Authored by Gayle Holdman
Illustrated as a collaborative effort by Dallin Orr and Irina Harding
Typography and original interior font by Desiree Rangel

Creative Director: Gayle Holdman
Production Supervision: Tom Holdman and Alan Knight

Text copyright ©2021 by Gayle Holdman
Illustrations copyright ©2021 Roots of Humanity Foundation
All rights reserved.
No part of this book shall be used or reproduced in any manner without written permission.
Limited Edition Printed in the United States of America.
For information, contact the publisher:
Roots of Humanity Foundation (a 501 (c)(3) nonprofit organization)
3001 N Thanksgiving Way, Suite 2, Lehi, UT 84043

info@rootsofhumanity.org
www.thepiecethatisyou.com

First (Limited) Edition: August 2021 (hb)

ISBN 978 1 7923 6905 6

The publisher is not responsible for websites, or the content thereof, that are not owned by the publisher.
Printed in China

For
humans everywhere
(younger and older),
that they may know
(and never forget)
how much they matter.

And to Mary, the very root of Roots.

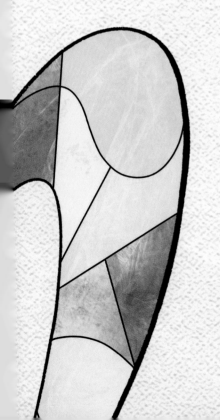

To access Animate Art

scan QR code

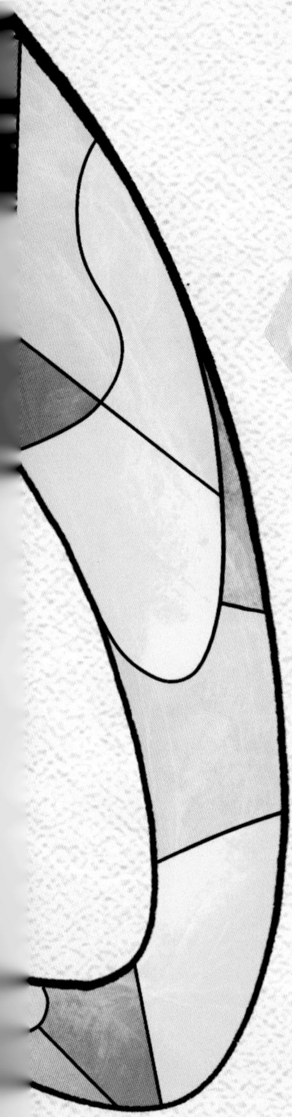

THE PIECE THAT IS YOU

Thank you for all the good you do with the piece that is you.

with much love
Gayle Holdman

BY

GAYLE HOLDMAN

ILLUSTRATED BY

DALLIN ORR

& IRINA HARDING

The world's a big place. It's easy to ask,
"Where do I fit in? What might be my task?"

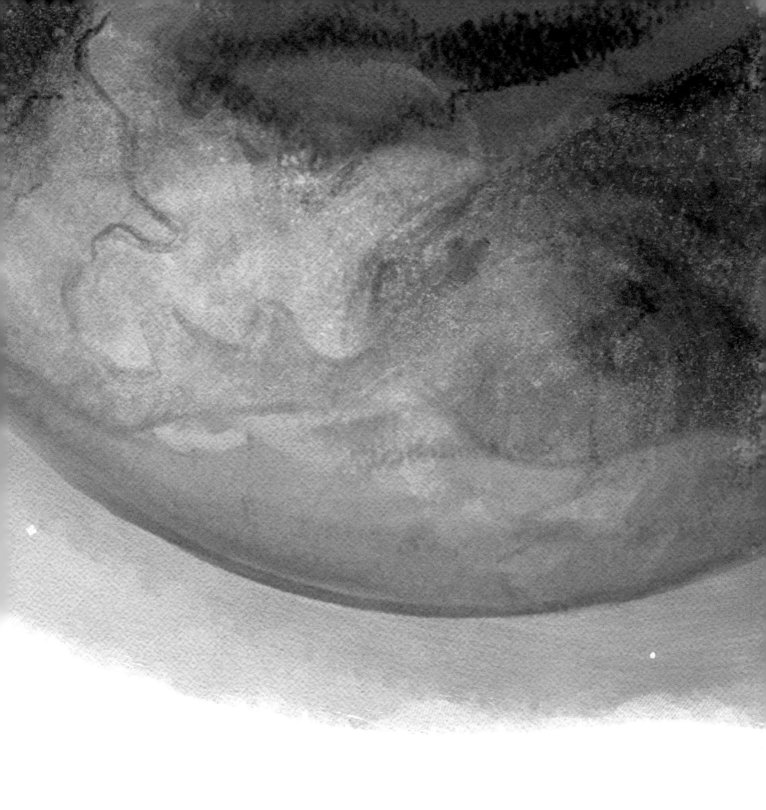

There was a boy who had those questions, too.
Look at what he was inspired to do.

He struggled to speak when he was still small.
At times, the boy could not say much at all.

It was hard. It hurt when he was ignored.
But there were more ways to speak he explored.

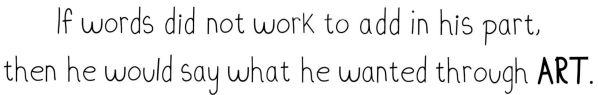

If words did not work to add in his part,
then he would say what he wanted through **ART**.

And that's what he did, each day of his life.
Art helped him to "speak" and lessened the strife.

One day on a bench in front of a school,

he got an idea so HUGE, BIG, and COOL.

It was *ginormous*: a SUPER-SIZE dream!
Now he would need a remarkable team.

It was way too big to do on his own;
it would be better if he weren't alone.

It's filled with events, people, and places.
(You may or may not know some of the faces.)

It has math and science, music and dance,
those who were willing to go take a chance!

So much to find! There are coins, trees, and birds,
and quotes that show the great power of words.

And people! From all over the world! See?
They're not that different from you or from me.

Lincoln brought freedom and a country together.
Clark and Lewis explored, whatever the weather.

Ruth's chocolate chip cookie: a treat to take along.
Joan of Arc, oh so faithful, courageous, and strong.

Shelley and Shakespeare, Doyle and Austen,
stories to be read and enjoyed often!

Merchant ships traveled with their heavy load.
(And why is that chicken there, crossing the road?)

Gandhi, Malala, and still hundreds more waiting for you to discover, explore!

Confucius and Plato both thought about light
and how happiness comes from doing what's right.

Tom Edison holds a star from Van Gogh.
There's Sesame Street and The Places You'll Go.

Da Vinci, Mandela and others from history
took their place in this world full of wonder and mystery.

Each made a difference; there's a place where they fit.
It might have been hard, but not one of them quit.

You're unique in this life; there's a spot just for you!
Never forget all the good *YOU* can do.

Like these pieces of glass, your color and size
matter less than if you are someone who tries.

Every piece of the window is different, it's true.
Big or small, each one matters. It's needed... like *YOU*!

We all have talents. We all have a gift.
Find ways to use yours to build and uplift.

Always be kind and work hard. Do your best.
Your life can brighten the lives of the rest.

Something awesome can come from what you do, too.
The world will be blessed by the **piece** that is **YOU!**

The piece that is Gayle:

Gayle

Growing up super shy and sensitive, Gayle knows what it feels like to wonder where you fit in. She also knows that miracles happen once you figure that out.

She really loves people and helping them see how amazing they are. To do that better, Gayle got an education in Human Development, Positive Psychology, and Spanish. Plus, she studies other languages and interesting stuff about humans every day. Working with stained glass has taught her even more about the importance of every single piece (person).

Gayle is grateful to live, write, and create at the foot of ginormous and beautiful rock-filled mountains. For fun, she adores cooking and paper crafting (but hates the clean-up!) The absolute most important pieces of her heart and life are her husband, Tom, and their three unique and precious children.

To learn more or to schedule an author presentation, visit: www.thepiecethatisyou.com

The Pieces that are the Boy and his Team:

This story is based on the real-life experiences of stained glass artist, Tom Holdman (Gayle's husband). He began stuttering as a child and had to learn other ways to express himself. The idea for Roots actually did come while he was sitting on a bench of a local university. The enormous mural took a long time to design and fabricate requiring lots of effort from lots of people. Many thanks to Utah Valley University for participating in its creation. And huge thanks to the gifted and hard-working team at Holdman Studios. Stained glass is a tedious and labor intensive medium; we couldn't do what we do without you.

See more from Holdman Studios at www.holdmanstudios.com

Tom and his team

Roots of Knowledge Gallery

The Piece that is Dallin:

As a child, Dallin loved to draw, especially things like monsters, planets, and dinosaurs. He also wanted to be an astronaut. Ultimately, he followed his gift and passion for creativity and ended up earning a Masters of Fine Art in Illustration.

Beginning as a student intern, Dallin quickly became one of the lead artists for the Roots of Knowledge project. He has now been a part of the Holdman Studio's team for six years.

Dallin loves learning about history and philosophy, going rock climbing, and jamming with his band. Sometimes you'll find him making bleeps and bloops with his electronic music equipment.

To see more of his work visit www.dallinorr.com

Dallin and Irina

The Piece that is Irina:

Irina has always loved drawing and art. Now, she also loves to teach art to children. She's passionate about seeing and encouraging the creativity children naturally possess.

Born in Russia, Irina moved to the United States when she was 21. It was challenging to live in a different culture, speaking a different language, and still can be. Nevertheless, she loves new experiences, meeting new people, and exploring the world, through books, movies, and travel.

Some of the most important pieces of Irina's life are her family, including her husband, five children, two step-children, two dogs, two cats, two parakeets, and four chickens. She loves getting out in nature, especially hiking or camping.

Irina is working towards a degree in illustration from Utah Valley University. You can see more of her work on behance and instagram. She loves children's books and hopes this book will spark creativity in everyone who reads it.

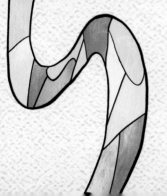

The end of this story,
and the beginning of yours...